More
Little
Stories for
Little Children

By the Same Author
Little Stories for Little Children
(Herald Press, 1995)

More
Little
Stories for
Little Children

A Worship Resource

Donna McKee Rhodes

HERALD PRESS
Scottdale, Pennsylvania
Waterloo, Ontario

Library of Congress Cataloging-in-Publication Data
Rhodes, Donna McKee, 1962-
    More little stories for little children : a worship resource /
Donna McKee Rhodes.
      p. cm.
    ISBN 0-8361-9059-9 (alk. paper)
    1. Children's sermons. 2. Storytelling in Christian
education. I. Title.
BV4315.R47 1996
252'.53—dc20   96-32340
                                                CIP

The paper used in this publication is recycled and meets the minimum requirements of American National Standard for Information Sciences—Permanence of Paper for Printed Library Materials, ANSI Z39.48-1984.

MORE LITTLE STORIES FOR LITTLE CHILDREN
Copyright © 1997 by Herald Press, Scottdale, Pa. 15683
    Published simultaneously in Canada by Herald Press,
    Waterloo, Ont. N2L 6H7. All rights reserved
Library of Congress Catalog Number: 96-32340
International Standard Book Number: 0-8361-9059-9
Printed in the United States of America
Cover art and book design by Paula M. Johnson

05 04 03 02 01 00 99 98 97 10 9 8 7 6 5 4 3 2 1

To the children of
Stone Church of the Brethren,
whose lively and wonder-filled
presence adds a rich dimension
to our congregational life.

Contents

Preface and Acknowledgments

*A*S WAS THE CASE WITH MY PREVIOUS collection of stories, *Little Stories for Little Children* (Herald Press, 1995), I hope this new set will contribute to your ministry with children, whether in a worship time, church school classroom, camp setting, or family home. Use the stories as they are or as a springboard for your own ideas. These stories result from continued ministry with the children of Stone Church of the Brethren. All of the stories have been developed to match a scriptural or worship theme in our services.

I am thankful for my staff colleagues, Pastor Dawn Ottoni Wilhelm and Judy Cooper, administrative secretary. Our times of shared ministry deepen our commitment to service as God wills. Many folks in the Stone Church congregation provide on-going encouragement in my writing endeavors for which I am grateful. My husband, Loren, provided valued computer assistance in preparing the manuscript, and my children were great "story idea testers."

I am grateful to Herald Press for inviting me to put this second collection of stories together and to Michael King for being a thoughtful editor. Thank you to the thousands of readers who found the earlier stories helpful. I hope you enjoy these new stories as well.

—*Donna McKee Rhodes*
Huntingdon, Pennsylvania

*I*ntroduction

WHAT A GIFT GOD has given to us in children. Their smiles, their enthusiasm for life, their love of fun, their wonderment at realizing what to them is a new revelation, and their sincere devotion to God can be inspirations and models for us as adults. And what responsibility God has given us as parents, teachers, and pastors to nurture children along their way!

This book is designed as a resource for that nurturing process. In these pages you will find a collection of fifty-two Scripture-based lessons intended for use in homes, church camp settings, worship services, or any other appropriate settings.

The stories are not rigidly tied to the church year but do loosely follow it. Thus storytellers looking for stories for special church days—such as Palm Sunday, Easter, Christmas—will find them about where they would expect if treating the stories as tied to weeks of the year.

The majority of these stories are designed to use easy-to-find objects which help teach a scriptural concept. The use of objects with which children are familiar and can identify helps children move from the known (the object they can relate to) to the unknown (the Scripture concept.)

Although most stories use an object, a few do not. Several stories are rhythm poems which have a repetitive, responsive line for the children to say while the leader has more to say. A couple of stories are simple skits which require the help of a few children.

Some stories incorporate a simple game to help teach the concept. A number of stories close with the children being given some small item such as a picture, a sticker, or a food item. All the stories can be shared with a minimum of preparation and expense.

The stories are not lengthy. I believe only one point should be made during this short time with the children. An interlude with children during a worship service is not a time to remake all the points in the sermon. Rather, this time is for the children to learn of God's love for them and his constant presence in their lives as well as to feel they are important members of their church family.

An added benefit of short story times is that opportunity for poor behavior and disruption is reduced. A lengthy story time during which children become restless can disrupt an entire worship service.

You may note recurring themes throughout this collection. It is helpful for children to hear basic concepts repeated at different times so they understand and incorporate these principles in their lives.

If you do story time on a regular basis, be aware if children in your group have special needs. Is there a child who for medical reasons may have difficulty with a food item? Are there children with visual or hearing problems? What about a child with a learning disability? It is good to have open communication with parents to be aware of potential issues.

If you feel you need a parent to sit with the children as you tell the story, ask someone to help. That will free you to give your attention to the entire group and to focus on maintaining a worshipful atmosphere.

Enjoy the time you spend with the children. Take seriously the responsibility God has given to us to nurture the children in our midst. As you minister to the children, let them minister to you through their smiles, excitement, and love for life!

More
Little
Stories for
Little Children

1

Brand-New Opportunities

Theme   Our New Year Holds New
   Opportunities
Scripture   Isaiah 43:19
Object   New crayons

GOOD MORNING! Today is a special day. New Year's Day! *(Or adjust this sentence to say that New Year's Day will occur this coming week.)* During this new year of _____ we have 365 new days *(in leap year, 366 days)*. Each one of those days is a special gift from God. We don't know what will happen during the days of _____, but each new day is a gift to us.

Our new year is like a new box of crayons. Do you like to draw? Isn't it special to have new crayons? When crayons have been used a lot they get to be yucky. The points aren't sharp. Sometimes the papers tear. Sometimes the crayons break into pieces. Isn't it exciting to get a new box of crayons? They are brand-new; each has a sharp point and is in one piece.

Our new year is like a new box of crayons. Even better, each new day is like a new box of crayons. Each day is a brand-new gift from God. There will be new things to learn and new people to be friends with. There will be ways we show that God lives in our lives.

If we have a bad day, we know a new day is right around the corner. The best part of each new day is that God is with us. God is with us no matter where we are or what we are doing.

This morning I have new crayons for each of you. As you use these crayons, remember that we not only have this new year; each day is also a new start and a wonderful gift from God to us.

Let's pray:

Dear God, thanks for our new year. Be with us during each new day. Thanks for the gifts you give us each day. Amen.

2
A New Start

Theme   God Gives Us New Beginnings
Scripture   Isaiah 1:18
Object   Snow or picture of snow

This story was done during a morning worship which included a service of baptism. The paragraph regarding the baptism can be deleted to fit your setting better.

GOOD MORNING! It's wintertime! How can we tell? The past week was very cold. We had snow and ice. Do all of you like snow? What do you like to do in the snow?

Snow can be pretty when it is fresh. The land during winter looks dark, and there are no fall leaves or summer flowers or green grass to give color to our world. But when the snow has just fallen, it gives everything a fresh, new look.

Each new day is a fresh beginning. That is a wonderful gift from God. When we say, "Jesus, I believe in you, and I want your Spirit to live inside of me," it is a new beginning. Our lives become clean, just like a fresh-fallen snow. Even when we do things that are not right, God can help our lives become clean again when we ask forgiveness.

Those of you who stay in our service after the story will see a time of baptism. When you become a little older, you will each have the opportunity to be baptized. Baptism is a wonderful new beginning, too.

A special thing about God is that he gives us new beginnings. It is good that God gives us many ways to make new beginnings. God shows his love for us in so many ways. We have new days. As we grow older, we get to try new things. And our lives can feel new when we ask God to forgive us. God is wonderful and forgiving. God will give us new starts over and over, every time we ask.

Let's pray:

Dear God, thank you for new beginnings. Thank you for loving us so much that you are always willing to give us new beginnings. Thank you for making our lives clean. Amen.

3

I n God's Image

Theme   We Are All Made in the Image of God
Scripture   Genesis 1:26-27
Object   Silly Putty, comic strips

GOOD MORNING! I would guess that at least some of you like to draw, paint, or do some other kind of craft. Do all of you like to create things? When we make crafts, we have pictures or ideas in our minds that we want to create. Then we work to put those ideas into forms such as drawings, paintings, or pieces of pottery.

I brought a page of comic strips with me today. Each of these comics started as an idea or an image in the creator's mind. Then she or he put those images on paper.

I also brought Silly Putty with me. Have you ever played with Silly Putty? *(Demonstrate how Silly Putty picks up the image of the comic strip.)* The putty picks up the image. It reflects the image. Isn't that interesting? Let's try it again with this comic strip. *(Pick another strip.)* It did it again!

When God created our world, God had some ideas in mind. God created the parts of nature—mountains, sun, water, birds, and many other things. Then God created people. The Bible tells us God created us in God's image. That means God copied us from God's own self! We certainly are not as powerful as God, but we are made in the image of God. Each of us is made in the image of God.

We saw how the Silly Putty reflects the image of the comic strip. Each of us reflects God because we are made in God's image. As we live each new day in our lives, we should try to let our words and actions reflect the image of God.

Let's pray:

Dear God, thank you for your wonderful creation. Help us to be good reflections of you. Amen.

$O^{\,4}_{\,nly\;God}$

Theme   God Should Be Number One
Scripture   Exodus 20:3-6
Object   Four-leaf clover or picture of one

*H*AVE ANY OF YOU lain on the grass in the summer and searched for a four-leaf clover? *(Adjust this paragraph to talk about your clover or your picture.)* I have often looked for a four-leaf clover but have never found one. A lot of people say a four-leaf clover will bring you good luck. I have a four-leaf clover I didn't find in the grass. I can't remember how I got this; I think someone mailed it to me. The paper it's wrapped in says, "Good Luck." I didn't save this clover because I thought it would bring me luck. Actually, I saved it because I knew someday I could use it during our story time.

Some people have special objects or habits that they think bring luck. Some people wear special socks they think bring good luck. Some wear special pieces of jewelry. Some cross their fingers or do something else they believe is lucky.

It's fun to think about a special object or habit, but the best thing to do is remember that we have God in our lives. God should be more important to us than a good luck charm. We can't treat God as a good luck charm. But we know God wants to have a special place in our lives. Trusting God to be with us every minute of every day is great!

We know God is with us. We know we can talk to God any time we want through prayer. We know God cares about everything that is happening in our lives. Our personal relationship with God is much more important in our lives than a four-leaf clover.

Let's pray:

Dear God, we're glad you want to be first in our lives. Thank you that each one of us is special to you. Amen.

5

*H*ow Is Your Memory?

Theme   Remember What God Has Done
  for You
Scripture   Deuteronomy 4:9-14
Object   Bowl of fruit

*L*ET'S PLAY A GAME together. I have a bowl of
fruit with me this morning. In the bowl are
_____. *(Name the items in your bowl. I used five
fruits—apple, orange, grapefruit, banana, grapes).* You
need to look carefully. Can everyone see? You need to
remember what fruits are in this bowl.

I'm going to take away a piece. Then let's see who
can remember what piece is missing. Ready? Close
your eyes, and don't peek! *(Remove one piece of fruit at a
time. Ask the children to guess what is missing. Repeat this
several times. As they correctly guess what fruit is missing,
praise them for being good at remembering.)*

That was fun! All of you were good at remembering what fruit was in the basket, then knowing what
fruit was missing.

It's good for us to remember things well. All of you
are learning to remember good manners and what is
right or wrong. Many of you are learning things in
school that are important to remember.

It's important for us to remember that God has given all of us many things to be thankful for. God has given us families and other people who care deeply for us. We all have food, clothes, and houses. God loves each one of us very much. We need to remember all those special things God has done for us.

As you grow older, there will be many things in your lives to remember. But never forget that God loves each one of us very much. Remember to say, "Thank you, God."

Let's pray:

Dear God, thank you for all you have done for us. Thank you for all of your gifts to us. Help us to remember you in everything we do. Amen.

6

*L*et's Make a Deal

Theme We Have Many Choices to Make
Scripture 1 Samuel 8:4-20
Object Stickers, cookies hidden in a box

GOOD MORNING! I have a game to play together. This game is called "Let's Make a Deal." *(This is an activity children really enjoy. Go slowly through the choices because there are several questions.)*

I am going to give you a choice. You can have a nice sticker or you can choose what is in this box. You don't know what's in the box. It could be something really nice. Maybe it's something to eat. Maybe it's something fun. Maybe it's something awful. Maybe there's nothing in this box at all.

You need to decide: Are you going to trust that you'll like what is in this box, or are you going to take the sticker you can see? That's a lot to think about, isn't it?

How many of you want a sticker? How many of you choose what's in the box, even though you don't know what is in the box?

Do you really trust me? What if something hops out of the box?

Okay, let's look at what is in the box. *(I had cookies in*

it.) Something good to eat! Cookies! Are you glad you chose the box? After our prayer, you can each have a sticker and a cookie.

You had to make a choice just now. You needed to decide if you wanted the sticker or if you trusted me not to be playing a trick on you with an empty box or a box with something awful in it.

All during our lives we need to make decisions. We need to make decisions at school and at home. You need to make decisions when you are playing with your friends. As you grow up, there will be lots of decisions to make.

Sometimes we make right decisions. Sometimes we make bad decisions. But we know God loves us through whatever decisions we make. God might not be happy if we make bad decisions, but God will always love us.

One decision that is always right is deciding to trust in God. When you put trust in God's constant presence, love, and guidance, you're making a great decision.

We can trust that God will help us make good decisions. God wants us to trust him; trusting God is a wonderful choice to make.

Let's pray:

Dear God, as we face many decisions in our lives, help us to always trust in you. Remind us of your constant love and guidance. Amen.

7
S torm Clouds

Theme   God Helps Us When Our Lives Feel
  Stormy
Scripture   Psalm 27:1-9
Object   Pictures of storm clouds and of blue sky

GOOD MORNING! I brought a couple of pictures
to show you. The first is of clouds. *(Show picture
of storm clouds.)* What do these clouds look like?
They're dark. They look scary. They look like a storm
will soon be happening.

Are any of you scared during a storm? Do thunder
and lightning scare you? What helps you feel calmer
through a storm? *(Affirm their answers.)*

Sometimes things happen in our lives that are
scary or make us feel sad. These times can feel like
storms. Maybe we get sick and feel bad. Maybe you
have a disagreement with a brother or sister or friend.
You may feel angry with each other. Maybe something
sad has happened like your pet died or you did not get
to do something special you had planned.

Any of those times can make you feel sad or scared
or angry. Those times are like a storm with dark
clouds.

But what happens after a storm? Do the dark

clouds stay? No. *(Show picture of blue sky.)* The sky becomes blue. Just as the sky changes from stormy to blue, when you're sad or scared you can begin to feel better because God is with you.

Sometimes God helps us through other people. Parents and friends who care about us help us feel better.

God always cares about how we are feeling, whether we are happy or sad or scared. God is with all of us, helping us and comforting us.

Remember, you can always tell God how you feel, and God will understand.

Let's pray:

Dear God, thanks for caring about us and understanding our feelings. Thank you for helping us when we are scared or sad or angry. Amen.

G⁸od's Voice

Theme   Listen and Look Carefully for God's
Voice
Scripture   Psalm 29
Object   Tape player, tape with various sounds

(Before story time, prepare a tape with five or six common sounds the children will recognize—TV, alarm clock, etc.)

GOOD MORNING! Let's play a game. I'm going to play a tape with sounds recorded on it. They're sounds you hear at your house. You have to listen carefully. You need to be very quiet and still.

As soon as you know the sound, tell me. Ready? Let's listen. *(Play the tape. Affirm their efforts.)*

You did well! You were good listeners. You knew that to identify what the sound was you needed to be quiet and listen carefully.

We need to listen very carefully in our lives to hear God's voice. That is kind of hard to understand as children because you know that God is not sitting here as a person talking with us as we are.

But we do know God's Spirit is with us wherever we are. God always listens when we pray. And God does talk to us.

We might not always hear that talk just like we hear each other's talk. But sometimes we may sense that God says something to us when we pray. We may hear God through our friends. We may hear God through the sounds of nature, such as wind, rain, or thunder.

Sometimes, God may use us as his voice. When we talk with other people, our words and actions tell them about God.

You listened carefully to the taped sounds. Listen and look carefully in your lives, and you will hear God's voice.

Maybe you will hear God's voice when you pray. Maybe you will hear God when you are outside enjoying nature. Maybe you will hear God when you are with your family and friends.

And remember, when you speak and do things, other people may be seeing God's love and hearing God's voice through you.

Let's pray:

Dear God, thank you for your constant presence in our lives. Help us to be good listeners so we will hear your voice. Help us to be good speakers and "do-ers" so other people see your love and hear your voice through us. Amen.

9

Supportive Connections

Theme   Family Members Support One
   Another
Scripture   Ruth 1:16-17
Object   Box of pop-up tissues

GOOD MORNING! I brought a box of tissues with me today.

Winter is the season for lots of colds and sneezes, right? I don't have a cold today, so that is not the reason I brought the tissues. I want to show you something about tissues.

Someone take a tissue. What happened? There's another tissue available right away. Let's try it again. There's one ready to be taken again. Does anyone else need a tissue?

How does this work? Does the first tissue pull the next one out? Do the tissues in the box push one up to be ready? The tissues support one another.

In our families, we support one another. We are in relationships together. There are times a member of a family may need more support than at other times.

Maybe that person has been sick or sad about something. Then as a family we can help that person with extra love and care. We support that person.

Sometimes you might be the person in the family who needs help. Then you can count on your family to help and support you with love and care.

We have relationships with friends and church family, too. Sometimes we give support in those relationships. Sometimes we receive support. When we are part of the family of God, we should be willing to love, support, and care for others.

It's good to know we can count on love and support in our family. There is a tissue ready in the box which is our family!

Let's pray:

Dear God, thanks for our families. Thanks for the love we share, not only with our families, but also with our friends and church family, too. Amen.

10

*W*e Are All Travelers

Theme   We Travel with God All of Our Lives
Scripture   Ezekiel 34:11-16
Objects   Toy vehicles

I BROUGHT SOME toys with me today. These toys all have something in common. Tell me when you know what it is they have in common. *(Each toy represents a way to travel. Adjust the next paragraph to match your toys.)*

I have a space shuttle. Here is a car. This toy is a truck. Here is a little bike. Do you know what they have in common? *(Wait for a response. We hope the children will say the toys represent ways to travel.)*

That's right. These toys are vehicles. They show ways we can travel. People can travel in cars, trains, and planes. Can you think of other ways people can travel? *(Roller blades, skis)*

People travel in many ways. We named a lot of them just now. There is another way we as Christians travel. All of our lives we travel with God. All of life is a journey. Some people say we walk with God. God is with us always.

It is good to know that God is with us every minute of every day and night. As we travel on our journeys with God, we try to live our lives doing things that make God happy.

We try to live by the rules in the Bible. Each of us makes mistakes on our journeys. We might even make a lot of mistakes. But we know God forgives us when we are sorry. We can talk to God through prayer any time we want on our journey.

Someday, our traveling on these journeys will be over when we are in heaven and see God face-to-face. But for now, we can do our best to travel in a good and safe way with God beside us!

Let's pray:

Dear God, we're all traveling on journeys with you throughout our lives. Guide us on our journeys. Help us to live our lives the way you want us to. Thank you for being with us as we travel. Amen.

11

*O*ur First-Aid Kit

Theme   How Can We Be More Like Jesus?
Scripture   Galatians 6:7-10
Object   Tongue depressor, cloth, Band–Aids,
   tape, peroxide

HOW MANY OF YOU have a first-aid kit in your house or car? A lot of you do. What are some things in a first-aid kit? *(Wait for their responses.)*

We know that first-aid items are important when somebody has an accident and needs care. It's important to have the items ready to help the hurt person.

Not only do we need care for our physical bodies, but we need care for our spirits. We are beginning a season of the church year called Lent. During this season we think about what it means to follow Jesus. We think about how we can be more like Jesus.

To help us think about those things, I have a spiritual first-aid kit with me today.

First, I have a tongue depressor. Sometimes our tongues and our mouths say things that are not nice or true. A tongue depressor reminds us to watch our words! We should use careful words that will not make someone feel sad.

Next, I have a bottle of peroxide. Has your mom or

dad ever put peroxide on a cut? The peroxide bubbles and makes the area of the cut clean. It cleans away germs. God makes us clean. God can make our spirits clean when we ask.

Then we have a washcloth. A washcloth makes us clean. We should have clean thoughts and actions.

Here are some Band-Aids. A Band-Aid covers a sore spot when we get hurt. But you know, words can hurt our feelings. Kind words can help people feel better. We should let our kind words cover and heal other people's sad feelings.

Here's a roll of tape. This tape holds pieces of a gauze bandage together and keeps the bandage on the skin if we get really bad cuts. In our lives, prayer can help to hold us together. Talking to God through prayer can make us feel stronger.

After our prayer together, I am going to give each of you a Band-Aid. You can save this Band-Aid for sometime when you have a cut. But until then, let the Band-Aid remind you that our spirits need care, too. During this season of Lent, let's look at our lives and see what we can do to be more like Jesus.

Let's pray:

Dear God, we want to be more like you. Show us what we need to do in our lives to be more like you. Amen.

N12ew Life

Theme   New Life in Our World and for Us
Scripture   2 Corinthians 5:17
Object   Someone to draw a picture during story

(Have someone make a simple drawing of flowers, grass, butterflies, and other signs of spring as you talk. Practice the story and drawing together for timing.)

GOOD MORNING! As we talk, *(name of person)* will draw a picture about new life. Can you watch and listen at the same time? Let's try!

It's spring! How do we know? *(Encourage the children to tell you about signs of spring.)*

The grass is turning green. The leaves are beginning to appear on trees. We see flowers. There are baby animals. We see new life all around. Soon we will see butterflies. The butterflies changed from being caterpillars into butterflies. That is a sign of new life.

There are other signs of new life for us to see. People are planting flowers and vegetables because it is warm enough for the seeds to grow. The warm temperatures allow us to wear light clothes. It is staying lighter longer each day, so we can be outside in the evenings.

Not only does God give our world signs of new life, but God gives each one of us new life. Every day is new life for us. Each day is a new gift. Sometimes we do wrong or mean things to other people. But God forgives and still loves us. That is new life for us. We have new life when we say we believe in Jesus and want to live our lives showing that we follow Jesus.

The picture shows signs of new life—butterflies, a tree, flowers, and a blue sky. Our world is showing signs of new life during this season of spring. Look around and see these signs of new life. But also look at yourself because God is your new life every day!

Let's pray:

Dear God, thank you for all the signs of new life in our world. Thank you, too, for the new life you give to each one of us. Amen.

13
*P*alm Sunday

Theme Use Your Hands to Serve Jesus
Scripture Mark 11:1-11
Object Palms

*T*ODAY IS A SPECIAL DAY! It is Palm Sunday!
*(Remove the next sentence if not appropriate for your
setting.)* Many of you walked up the church aisle carrying palms this morning. Today we remember another
day long ago. We remember when Jesus came to a
town.

The people knew they were seeing a great king and
they wanted to honor him.

They said, "Hosanna! Blessed is he who comes in
the name of the Lord!"

They honored Jesus by waving palms. Some people even took off their coats and laid them on the
ground for Jesus to ride over on his donkey. The people were excited to see Jesus.

Palms were important to the people who lived
when Jesus did. They used palms for many different
things. Sometimes they tied bunches of palms together
and used them to make roofs for their houses. Sometimes, because the palms are strong, they wove them
together to make mats, baskets, ropes, even sandals.

There are other palms that are important. They are the palms of our hands. Our hands are important. We can use our hands to help other people. When we help other people, we are honoring Jesus.

Maybe we give handshakes. Maybe hugs. Maybe we help with a job. Maybe we give food. In whatever way we help by using our palms, we honor Jesus. Just as the people long ago honored Jesus by waving palm branches, we can find ways to honor Jesus by using the palms of our hands.

Let's pray:

Dear Jesus, thanks for our hands, for our palms, that we can use to honor you. May we always remember you with honor and praise. Amen.

14

*T*he Empty Tomb

Theme   The Empty Tomb Is a Great Gift
Scripture   Mark 16:1-8
Object   Wrapped present

HAPPY EASTER! This is a special day! Sometimes we celebrate special days, such as birthdays and Christmas, with presents. Because Easter is such a special day, I brought a present along with me.

I need someone to open it so all of us can see it. *(Have someone open the present.)*

What's in it? Nothing? It's empty. Wow, what a present! An empty box. An empty box may seem to be a strange present, but it has a special meaning. This empty box reminds us of another empty space that was a present to us.

Long ago, on the Sunday morning after Jesus died, the women went to the tomb where Jesus' body was kept. They wanted to prepare his body for burial. But when they got to the tomb, it was empty.

The women were surprised and scared. They wondered what happened to Jesus' body. They were afraid someone had stolen the body of Jesus.

An angel told the women that Jesus was not in the tomb. The angel told the women that Jesus had risen.

The women became scared and hurried on their way to tell other people about Jesus' resurrection.

That empty tomb is a wonderful gift to us. Jesus had risen and he lives for us today. Because of the empty tomb and Jesus' resurrection, we have hope, we have life, and we have Jesus in our lives! That is a wonderful gift!

Let's pray:

Dear God, thank you for that empty tomb long ago on the first Easter morning. Thank you that Jesus is in our lives. Amen.

15
*W*e Are Gifts

Theme   We're Gifts and Can Give Our Talents
  as Gifts
Scripture   Isaiah 6:8
Object   Gift boxes drawn on papers.

(Preceding story time, prepare a sheet of paper with a gift box drawn on it for each child.)

GOOD MORNING! Tell me, do all of you like to receive gifts? *(Expect a joyful response!)* I knew it!

We all like to receive gifts. There are gifts at Christmas time. There are gifts at birthdays and other special occasions. Sometimes the gifts are wrapped in a pretty way with nice paper and a bow. Sometimes the gifts are in pretty bags. It's special to get and give gifts.

Do you know each one of you is a gift? We're all gifts, because God made each of us special. God gave each of us gifts. God gave us not only our families, friends, and God's love, but God gave us talents and abilities to do some things well.

Some people sing or play a musical instrument. Other people have a good attitude. Some people have the gift of caring for others. Some people are good artists or teachers.

It's up to us to learn what special talents God gave us. We can use those talents to honor God. When we do that, we're giving a gift to God. That's a special thing to do.

After our prayer, I'll give each of you a piece of paper with a big gift box drawn on it. Think what you do well. Can you use that to honor God? Write about what you do well or draw a picture of what you do well. Let that be your gift to God.

Let's pray:

Dear God, thank you for your gifts to us. Help us learn what we do well. Guide us as we let that be our gift to you. Amen.

16
A Great Strength

Theme With God in Our Lives, We Are Strong
Scripture Isaiah 40:31
Object Piece of string and braided yarn

(Ahead of time, braid three pieces of yarn into a length of about ten inches. Bring a string of the same length.)

I NEED A VOLUNTEER who has really strong muscles. Do you think you can break this string? *(Volunteers are eager to try! Pick one person.)*

You do? Let's see. Wow! You were able to break the string! That didn't look hard at all. That string was easy to break.

Now I need another strong volunteer. This job is harder. Do you think you can break this braided yarn? Do you want to try? It will be hard. Can't do it? What if you hold one end and I pull on the other? We still can't do it. This yarn is stronger because it's braided and woven together.

A verse in the Bible says, "Those who wait on the Lord shall renew their strength, they shall mount up with wings like eagles, they shall run and not be weary, they shall walk and not faint."

If we don't let God into our lives, we're like the

string that's easily broken. But when we let God in our lives, we're strong like the braided yarn. God weaves strength into our lives.

Talking to God through prayer, learning about God through reading and listening to Bible stories, and coming to church are things that help us to know more about God so we can be strong in our lives.

Even though God is in our lives, there will still be times when we feel hurt or sad. But because God is with us, we can be strong like the braided yarn. God gives us strength for our lives. If we begin to feel weak, we can always build that strength as we pray to and trust in God.

Let's pray:

Dear God, thank you for your great strength! Thank you for the strength you put in our lives! Help us to always trust in you. Amen.

$W^{17}_{e\ Believe}$

Theme   We Believe in God and God's Help
Scripture   Isaiah 43:10
Object   Seeds, a packet of seeds for each child

(Ahead of time, tape four types of seeds to index cards and label each seed card with the correct name. Keep them in your pocket.)

GOOD MORNING! Do you know what a miracle is? Have any of you heard that word in church school or anywhere else? *(Wait for response.)*

Yes, a miracle is something amazing that happens —something very special.

I have some miracles with me. Can you believe that? *(Pull a card one at a time from your pocket.)*

This seed is a miracle. It's going to grow into a radish.

This seed is a miracle. It will grow to be a carrot.

This seed is a miracle. It will grow a pumpkin vine.

This seed is a miracle. It will grow into a marigold.

How many of you help to plant seeds at your house? When we plant seeds, we need to give them a lot of care. We need to cover them with soil. We need to water them. The sun helps them grow. We believe that God will help them grow. We believe God does the miracle of helping the seeds change into plants.

We can believe that God helps us too. Each of us is growing. You're not only getting bigger, but you're growing in understanding and believing in God.

You know how the seeds need sun, soil, and water to grow? We need things too. We need people who care about us. Family, teachers, and our church family care.

We need to hear and read stories from the Bible and come to church to worship God. We need to look all around us and see God in the people and the world around us.

As we do these things, our belief and trust in God keeps growing.

After our prayer, I will give a packet of seeds to each of you. As you're growing and believing in God, plant these flowers, care for them carefully and watch them grow, too.

Let's pray:

Dear God, thank you for being all around us. Thank you for showing us reasons to believe in you. Help each of us as we grow and believe in you. Amen.

_18_
A Piece of Clay

Theme   God Helps to Shape Us
Scripture   Jeremiah 18:1-11
Object   Piece of clay

(Have a piece of clay to work in your hands as you speak.)

HOW MANY OF YOU like to play with clay? *(Expect a joyful response.)*

I thought most of you would like to play with clay. That's something most children enjoy. You can make all sorts of shapes with clay. You can roll it into a snake. You can make little balls or a larger ball. You can even shape the clay into a bowl.

There is a Scripture in the Bible, in the book of Jeremiah, which says that "Just like the clay in the potter's hand, so are you in my hand." God can help shape us just as a potter shapes a piece of clay.

That doesn't mean God changes our body shape. It does mean we should be willing to let God guide our lives. God has plans for us.

God hopes you'll pray and ask for guidance as you grow. Even adults pray to God and ask for guidance. When we ask God for help, we're letting God shape us. We're letting God guide and mold us into what

God wants us to be. We're saying to God that we trust the guidance God gives us.

We don't know what plans God has for us, but God does. Pray for guidance and be willing to follow God's leading as God shapes you and your lives.

Let's pray:

Dear God, sometimes it's hard to be patient and wait for answers. Guide and lead us. Shape us into what you want us to be. Amen.

19

The Gift of Baptism

Theme Baptism Is a Special Event
Scripture Matthew 3:13-17
Object Jar of water

I HAVE A JAR OF WATER with me this morning. What all can we do with water? *(Expect answers such as drink it, use it to clean, bathe in it, cook with it, swim in it, water the plants, make ice cubes.)* There are many uses for water and you named many of them.

There is a special service which we have sometimes in our church that uses water. Do any of you know what that special service is called? You're right. It's called baptism. Some of you may remember seeing a service of baptism.

There is a Scripture in our Bible that tells us of Jesus being baptized. Jesus wanted to be baptized by his cousin John. Jesus and John walked into the waters of the river Jordan.

The Bible tells us that something wonderful happened when John baptized Jesus. The Spirit of God came down from heaven as a dove, which is a lovely bird. And a voice from heaven was heard saying, "This is my Son, the Beloved, in whom I am well pleased."

At that point, Jesus knew he belonged to God. He

wanted to do the work of God.

Jesus walked into a river to be baptized in the water. We use water for baptism because it's a way of picturing becoming clean. Baptism is a time to get rid of old ways and become new and clean in following Jesus.

(If your church follows forms of baptism that do not fit details described here, change the description accordingly.)

When you are older, all of you will be able to decide about being baptized. It's a wonderful time when you can make a promise to follow Jesus and commit to be dedicated to the church.

But until that time, you can learn a lot about Jesus by listening in church school and our worship services as we sing, pray, and read from the Bible.

Let's pray:

Dear God, thank you for the wonderful stories in the Bible, such as the one that tells about Jesus being baptized. We pray that you will continue to bless each one of us as we continue to follow you. Amen.

20

A voiding Temptation

Theme Don't Get Caught by Temptation
Scripture Matthew 4:1-11
Object Picture of a spiderweb

*H*AVE ALL OF YOU seen a spider's web at some time? Most of you have seen one.

I brought a picture of a spiderweb to show you while we talk. A spider works carefully to weave the web. A lot of time goes into making a web. The spider moves from one point to another, all the while connecting the strings of the web together.

Why do spiders spin webs? *(Wait for responses.)* Yes, to catch flies and bugs and other insects to eat. They get caught in the web because they get too close to it. They fly into the web and stick to it because the web is sticky.

Many times we get tempted to do something we shouldn't. Sometimes we give in and do what we shouldn't. Then we feel caught. We feel like we're flies which have gotten too close to the spider's web and become stuck.

Sometimes friends at school try to get you to say something unkind about someone or to be mean in some other way. Maybe some of you who are older feel tempted to cheat on a test. Maybe you feel tempted to take something that doesn't belong to you.

Children aren't the only ones who feel tempted. Grownups feel tempted sometimes too. When we give into temptation, we know we've done wrong.

But even though God may not be happy that we've done wrong, God is always willing to forgive us. It's not always easy to live our lives just as God wants us to. Sometimes we're tempted and we make mistakes.

When we feel tempted, we can pray to God and ask God to help us to be strong. But when we give in and do wrong, God is always willing to forgive us and help us to be strong again.

Let's pray:

Dear God, when we feel tempted, help us to do what's right. But when we do make a mistake, thank you for forgiving us. Amen.

21
A **Strong Wind**

Theme The Spirit Moves Us
Scripture Acts 2:1-4
Object Wind chime

*T*HIS MORNING I brought something special to show you. *(Show wind chime. Adjust this paragraph to describe your wind chime.)*.

How many of you have gone to the ocean? Do you like to collect shells? I didn't make this; it was already made when I bought it. It's a wind chime made from a variety of shells. We keep it on our screened-in porch. Every once in a while, we hear the shells make a pretty sound when they touch one another.

What causes them to touch one another? *(The children will likely answer that someone needs to move them or the wind causes the sound.)* Usually they make the sound when the wind blows. Sometimes the wind is light and we hear just a little sound. Other times, the wind is strong and we hear a louder sound.

There is a story in the Bible about Pentecost. This was a special time when Jesus' special friends—the disciples—and many other friends were together. All of a sudden a sound like a rushing, strong wind blew into the room. It filled the house where they were.

That was very exciting! People knew something wonderful and glorious was happening. The Holy Spirit was coming to them.

The Spirit is with us too. We can't see the Spirit, just as we can't see the wind that blows the chime.

But we can feel the wind. We can feel the wind when it is strong and when the breezes are gentle. We know there is a wind when we hear the wind chime make sounds.

We can feel the Spirit that is always with us. Jesus promised that the Holy Spirit will always be with us.

Let's pray:

Dear God, thanks for the great stories in the Bible like the one about Pentecost. Thank you for the Spirit that is always with us even though we can't see it. Amen.

22
*F*ind *Shelter*

Theme   God Provides Us with Shelter
Scripture   Psalm 57:1
Object   Three pipe cleaners for butterfly

(While telling this story, fold three pipe cleaners into the shape of a butterfly. Fold one pipe cleaner into the middle of the butterfly's body. Add the other two pipe cleaners as wings. It's simple—but practice ahead of time.)

*T*HIS MORNING I would like to tell you a story about a butterfly. The butterfly had a black body. The butterfly's wings were yellow and orange. *(Adjust the colors of the butterfly to match the colors of your pipe cleaners.)*

The butterfly was really beautiful. The butterfly was having a great time during the late days of summer. It flitted from flower to flower. It especially enjoyed sitting on sunflowers growing in a garden. It also enjoyed resting in the warm sunshine.

One day, though, a storm raged. The wind became very strong and the butterfly had a hard time flying. It began to rain hard, and the butterfly had an even harder time. It flew to a tree and found shelter under leaves on a limb.

When the storm was over, the butterfly left the tree. It flew to the flowers and again enjoyed the warm sunshine.

Sometimes we may feel like we are in a storm. We may feel really sad about something. We may not feel well because of sickness. We may feel angry or feel upset because someone is angry with us. Those times can make our lives feel very stormy.

But like the butterfly which flew to shelter in a tree, we can find shelter in God. We can tell God how we're feeling. We know God will comfort and help us when we ask.

We can talk to God other times too, not just when we're having a hard time. God wants to hear about our happiness and joy, too. We're very blessed to have a God who cares when we're having good times and when we're having bad times. The comfort and shelter God can give us is great!

Let's pray:
Dear God, thanks for being in our lives. Thanks for caring about us and helping us with everything we do and feel. Amen

23

G od Is a Great Healer

Theme   We All Need Healing
Scripture   Mark 5:21-43
Object   Band-Aid

L ET ME SEE. In this group, does anybody have a Band-Aid this morning? Does anybody have a skinned knee or a sore finger? *(Wait for response.)*

Sometimes we get hurt and need first aid. Have you ever fallen and cut your knee? Have you cut your finger? Sometimes it really hurts!

When you get hurt, sometimes your mom or dad can help the injury. They clean the sore area and put some medicine on it. Sometimes a cut needs a Band-Aid. Sometimes a bigger injury needs to be wrapped in gauze or some other special bandage. Sometimes a nurse or a doctor needs to help.

Children often get scrapes and cuts. Adults sometimes get hurt, too. Sometimes we get sick and need to go to the doctor for medicine.

When we have been injured or feel sick, often we feel sad and sometimes lonely. I'm sure your parents help you feel better. A kiss, a hug, and some kind words can help.

There is something else that can make us feel better when we're sick and hurt. We can remember that God is with us always and cares about how we feel. We can put our trust in God's love and healing ways. God helps to heal us and make us feel better.

Let's pray:

Dear God, there are times in our lives when we need you to help us feel better and to heal us when we're hurt or not well. Thank you for your comfort and your healing ways. Amen.

24
Don't Be Piggy

Theme Share with Others
Scripture Mark 10:17-27
Object Piggy bank

GOOD MORNING! I brought a bank with me this morning. Do any of you have your own bank at your house? Some children keep their banks in their rooms.

Do you put money in your bank? Do you save your money? Do you spend it sometimes? Now here's a hard question. You don't have to answer it; just think about it. Do you ever use some of your money to help other people? Mmm, that's a tough question!

This bank looks like a happy and loving pig because it has a smile and a heart. *(Describe the piggy bank you've brought.)* We sometimes think pigs are a little selfish. They only look out for themselves. Each wants the most corn, the most water, and the best mud hole to play in.

Now I'm certainly not accusing any of you of being piggies. But it's important that we think of other people and their needs and feelings, too. We learn in the Bible that it's more blessed to give than receive.

We need to keep our eyes open to see how we can

share with others. There are many ways to share with other people. Certainly sharing money is one way, but sharing food, clothes, or other needed items are also good ways of caring for others.

It's good to care for ourselves, but we need to care for other people too. Look around. See what help you can give! Look around and think, "Where does God want me to give?"

Let's pray:

Dear God, we have each been given much. Help us to give to other people. Amen.

25

The Lion and the Lamb

Theme Live Together in Peace
Scripture Luke 6:27-31
Objects Picture of lion and lamb together

HOW MANY OF YOU have been to a zoo? What can you see at a zoo? *(Expect lots of answers. If no one mentions a lion, add that to the list.)*

What do you know about lions? They're big, strong, and roar loudly. Do you think they're wild? Do you think they're mean?

Have you been to a farm? What can you see at a farm? *(Again expect a lot of answers, but guide them to thinking about a lamb.)* What do you know about lambs? They appear to be quiet and gentle.

How do you think a lion and a lamb would get along? Do you think they would be enemies? Do you think they would hurt each other?

(Adjust this paragraph to match your picture of a lion and lamb. I used a Christmas card.) I want to show you a card that pictures a lion and a lamb together. The picture shows the lamb and lion lying peacefully together. Who can read the word on the card? Peace.

In our world there are all sorts of people. Some people are easier to like than others. Some people are more fun to be around than others. But it's important that we love one another, even those who don't seem very lovable to us.

God gives us great love. God expects us to share that love with other people.

This picture shows the lion and the lamb at peace with each other. Let's all try to be peaceful with one another and share God's love.

Let's pray:

Dear God, thank you for your love to each of us. Help us to be peaceful and love one another just as you love us. Amen.

26

*T*he Good Samaritan

Theme   Be Kind to One Another
Scripture   Luke 10:29-37
Object   Willing actors

(Prepare upper elementary children to be actors in this story. Give them copies of the story several days early so they can be familiar with it. Rehearse at least once before presenting the story publicly.)

DURING OUR STORY TIME, watch the older children as they act as the characters in this story. This is a story Jesus told one day when teaching.

A Jewish man was traveling on the road to Jericho when some bad men took his clothes, hurt him, and left him to die along the roadside. *(Have a child lie where the other children can see him or her.)*

A priest walked by the injured man but he did not stop to help the hurt man. The priest decided to keep walking. *(Another child walks past the child lying on the floor. Encourage the child to look but just keep on walking.)*

Another man came upon the injured man. Just like the priest, this man walked by the injured man and decided to not help him. He continued walking on his way. *(This child does the same as the previous child.)*

Then a third man saw the hurt man. This man was a Samaritan, not a Jew. Jews and Samaritans didn't get along. Those who had passed by the injured man were all Jews. If two Jewish men did not stop to help the suffering Jew, surely the Samaritan wouldn't.

But the Samaritan knew he should help. He knelt beside the man and cared for his injuries. He helped the man to a nearby inn, which is like a hotel, so he could rest and get better. The man even paid the money so that the injured man could rest there and receive medicine and food. *(This child kneels and pretends to help. Both children rise. With arms around each other's shoulders, they walk off to the side as though going to the inn.)*

Then Jesus said to the people who were listening to him teach, "Who was the neighbor to the injured man?" As you have listened to the story, who would you say was the neighbor to the injured man? Yes, the man who helped the injured man was the good neighbor. And Jesus said, "Go and do the same."

Jesus tells us to be kind to one another. Jesus tells us to be good neighbors to one another. How can we show kindness to others? *(Wait for the children to respond and affirm positive answers.)*

Let's put those things to work in our lives so we can be good neighbors to all we meet.

Let's pray:

Dear God, help us to help those who need our help. Thank you for showing us how we should help others. Amen.

27

Living with Disagreements

Theme Learning to Deal with Disagreements

Scripture Luke 12:49-53

Object Three varieties of Teddy Grahams or animal crackers

*T*ELL ME—how many of you like to eat Teddy Grahams *(or animal crackers)*? This box is honey Teddy Grahams. Sound good to you?

Let's pour them in a bowl. Do you notice they all look much the same? Let's look at this box of cinnamon Teddys. Do you see how their color is different?

Let's look at this box of chocolate Teddy Grahams. Let's mix all the Teddy Grahams. We have quite a variety now. There are different flavors, different colors, and different shapes of teddy bears.

Who likes the honey best? Cinnamon? Chocolate? Who likes all three?

It's fun to have a variety of Teddy Grahams. *(If you use animal crackers, try to have three different animal shapes. Talk about the shapes of the animals rather than the flavor of Teddy Grahams.)*

There are many kinds of people, too. It's good that people aren't all the same. If we were all the same, we would like to do the same things as everyone else.

Wouldn't it be boring if we all had the same hair color? If we looked exactly alike? If we all liked to do exactly the same thing?

But it's good that we're different. One thing that happens because we're different is that sometimes we have disagreements. Because we're not exactly alike, sometimes we disagree.

Sometimes we get angry with one another. Do you ever get angry with someone in your family? Maybe you want to play on the swing but your brother or sister wants to play ball. Maybe you eat the last apple and your brother or sister wants it. If you can't agree to share, you have a disagreement.

There are going to be times we disagree with each other. But the important thing is to know how to deal with the disagreements. Maybe you need to share. Maybe you need to walk away. Maybe you need to ask someone to help you. You can always ask God to help you deal with anger and disagreements.

If I told you I decided to take these Teddy Grahams *(or animal crackers)* home with me and not give any to you, how would you feel? Probably a little angry. You would disagree with my decision, wouldn't you?

Would you agree if I told you I decided to share them with you? After our prayer, I'll really be glad to share these Teddy Grahams with you!

Let's pray:

Dear God, thanks for the variety of people in our lives. It is good that we are different. When disagreements come between us, help us to work out the problems. Amen.

28
*Y*ou Are Invited

Theme   Jesus Invites Us to Follow Him
Scripture   Luke 14:7-14
Object   Invitation for each child

(For the invitation, I prepared a folded half-sheet with a picture of Jesus on the cover and "I invite you to follow me. Jesus" on the inside.)

GOOD MORNING! Tell me—do any of you like to receive mail? Is it fun to check the mailbox and see if you have received something? What do you like to receive? *(Expect answers such as pictures, magazines, letters. If the children do not say invitations, lead them to that thinking.)* Some adults don't really like to get mail because sometimes they get bills. Do you know what bills are? That's right. They are letters reminding us we need to pay some money. But, a really fun thing to get in the mail are invitations. Do you ever get invitations? Sometimes we get invited to parties or other special events.

Did you know that I have an invitation for you today? There is one for everyone! Who can read what the invitation says? *(Let a child read the invitation.)* Jesus invites you to follow him!

That is a great invitation to receive. Jesus wants each of us to follow him. We learn about what Jesus expects from each of us when we read the Bible, come to church school and worship, and listen to our parents and teachers. Jesus wants us to do some important things in our lives. Jesus wants us to pray and listen to Bible stories. Jesus wants us to be kind and thoughtful to other people. Jesus wants us to be loving and peaceful. And, Jesus wants us to follow him. Sometimes, doing those things is easy. Sometimes doing those things is hard. But accepting Jesus' invitation to follow him is the right thing to do!

Jesus invites us to follow him our entire lives. Do you know it is an honor to follow Jesus? Jesus invites all of us to follow him. It doesn't matter who you are or what your skin color is. It doesn't matter where you live. Jesus loves each one of us and wants us to follow him. What a great invitation!

Let's pray:

Dear God, thank you for letting Jesus be our guide in our lives. Help us always to follow what Jesus wants us to do. Amen.

29
*T*he Story of Zacchaeus

Theme   Being Fair and Honest
Scripture   Luke 19:1-10
Object   Actors, two robes, money bag or basket

(Prepare two mature children, perhaps upper elementary, to be actors in this story. Rehearse at least once. Give them the script several days early.)

GOOD MORNING! Our Bible is filled with wonderful stories! We can hear stories about Noah and the ark, David and Goliath, and the birth of Jesus.

One story is about Zacchaeus. Have all of you heard about Zacchaeus?

Zacchaeus was short. He may have been the shortest man in town. He was a tax collector. That meant people had to give him money to give to the king.

(The child playing Zacchaeus takes the money bag to storyteller, worship leader, or pastor and gives the impression of asking for the money. Contact them ahead of time!)

But did you know Zacchaeus kept some of the money for himself? *(Zacchaeus should pretend to put money in his pocket.)* The people were not happy with Zacchaeus. In fact, they did not like Zacchaeus one bit. They disliked him because he kept their money.

One day the townspeople heard that Jesus was coming to their town. This was a great day! Everyone wanted to see Jesus, so the people hurried to the road where Jesus was to walk. *(Encourage the children to pretend to look for Jesus.)*

Well, Zacchaeus wanted to see Jesus too. But because he was short he couldn't see. Taller people were blocking his view. So to see better, Zacchaeus climbed a tree. Then he could see over all the people. *(Child playing Jesus begins walking up the aisle.)*

The tree was the perfect place for Zacchaeus to watch for Jesus. *(Zacchaeus puts his hand above his eyes to look for Jesus.)*

When Jesus got to the tree where Zacchaeus was, he looked up and said, "Come down, Zacchaeus. I want to visit with you. I want to talk to you." *(Zacchaeus acts surprised!)*

Zacchaeus was surprised but quickly came down.

Zacchaeus and Jesus walked to Zacchaeus's house. As they talked, Zacchaeus said, "I haven't been fair in collecting money. I'll pay back the money I took unfairly. And I'll change my ways to be fair always."

Jesus said, "Zacchaeus, today is a great day. You have chosen what is right." *(Zacchaeus and Jesus walk away.)*

That's the story of Zacchaeus who changed his ways to become fair and honest.

Let's pray:

Dear God, in our lives we have many chances to be fair and honest. Help us to do a good job. Amen.

30
A Helpful Spirit

Theme We Leave Tracks As We Help One
Another

Scripture John 14:25-29

Object Fabric with footprints

*(This can be a fun activity to prepare ahead of time! Use a
large piece of light-colored material and three colors of wash-
able paint. Recruit a couple of children to help. In bare feet,
step in paint, then walk on the sheet. The feet will leave tracks
all over the fabric.)*

HOW MANY of you have seen animal tracks
outside? We can see tracks when we look closely. We see tracks in soil, sand, or snow. As we look really carefully, we can see what kind of animal made
those tracks by looking at the footprints.

I have another kind of tracks to show you today.
(Have helpers hold the fabric.) Do you know what kind of
tracks these are? People tracks. These people left
tracks because they had paint on the bottom of their
feet.

Do you know that wherever we go we leave tracks?
Sometimes, such as when we've stepped in paint for a
project like this, we can see the tracks. We can also see

them in snow. If you don't wipe your feet before going into the house, you might make tracks that won't make your parents happy. Those are tracks we can see.

But we also leave tracks that we can't see. Our actions leave tracks that we can't see. We hope to leave good tracks by doing good actions.

We can leave good tracks by being kind and peaceful with others. When we help someone, we're making good tracks. We hope we don't leave bad tracks by being mean and not thoughtful.

Sometimes it's hard to leave good tracks. But Jesus promises to help us. Jesus promises that the Holy Spirit will always be with us—helping, guiding, and teaching us. Jesus promises that the Holy Spirit will be with us forever to help us.

That is a very special promise. We can trust in Jesus' promise that the Holy Spirit will be with us always, guiding us and leading us on our paths.

Let's pray:

Dear Jesus, thank you for your promise of the Holy Spirit to be with us always. Thank you for that special helper for us. Amen.

31 _____
Firmly Attached

Theme   Stay Attached to God
Scripture   John 15:1-10
Object   A piece of a plant

(Choose a plant from which you can break a stem or branch without damaging the entire plant. I used an apple branch which still had blossoms. The main idea here is that the piece of plant can no longer grow when cut from its source. We too need to stay connected to God. Adjust the beginning paragraph to match your plant.)

HOW MANY of you like to eat apples? Do any of you like applesauce? How about apple pie? I have a branch of apple blossoms from a tree in our backyard. Apples eventually grow from the blossoms. The other delicious foods I just mentioned can be made from the apples.

What will happen to this branch? Do you think the blossoms will stay pretty? Will they eventually grow into apples?

No, because I've broken this branch from the tree. The blossoms need to be connected through the branch to the tree. The tree gives them water and nourishment.

We too need to be connected to our source of strength, which is God. God wants us to feel close to him. One way to feel close to God is through prayer. We can talk to or listen to God through prayer. We can talk to God about anything when we pray.

Another way to feel connected to God is through Scripture. When we listen to or read Bible stories and other parts of the Bible, we're learning how to live as Christians. We're learning how to be strong Christians.

Being with other Christians is also a great way to be strong and feel close to God. We support and encourage one another in our church family. We care about one another.

The branch needs to be connected to its source, the tree, to grow, be healthy, and produce fruit. The other branches on the tree will grow and the blossoms develop into fruit because they are still connected.

We need to be connected to God to grow into strong, healthy Christians. Prayer, Scripture, and fellowship with other Christians help us stay close to God

A special thing about God is that even though we may sometimes feel disconnected or broken away from God, God is always with us and willing to help us feel connected again.

Let's pray:

Dear God, we do want to grow into strong Christians and feel close to you. Help us remember that you are always close to us. Amen.

32
*W*hat Can I Give?

Theme We Can Give Ourselves and Our
Actions to God
Scripture John 12:1-3
Object No object, but practice a rhythm
pattern

I HAVE A RHYTHM POEM and I need you to help
me. We will say two sentences together: "What
can I give, O God? What can I give?" Let's practice that
together. *(Practice, then praise the children's efforts.)*

After those sentences, I'll say some other sentences. Each time I raise my hand, we'll all say the sentences we practiced again. Ready? Here we go!
Children: What can I give, O God? What can I give?
Leader: With each person I meet and with each thing I
do, I should be my very best and give the praise to you.
Children: What can I give, O God? What can I give?
Leader: I should give more than money. I should give
more than time.

The gifts you have given me are not just mine.
Children: What can I give, O God? What can I give?
Leader: The gifts you have given me are meant to be
shared,

To share with other people to show them I have cared.

Children: What can I give, O God? What can I give?

Leader: You have given much—our families and friends,

The beauty of the world to see and your love that never ends.

Children: What can I give, O God? What can I give?

Leader: Back to you I give a gift, I promise this you see:

To be the best that I can be in words, and thoughts, and deeds.

And so, dear God, my gift to you is—all of me!

Let's pray:

Dear God, thank you for giving so many wonderful things to us! We have families and friends, homes, and a pretty world. Help us to give ourselves to you, God. Amen.

33

A Church Is Not Just a Building

Theme People Make the Church
Scripture 1 Peter 2:4-5
Object Picture of your church building

(Find a picture of your church building.)

I HAVE A PICTURE to show you this morning. Do you recognize this building? You're right! It's a picture of our church building.

(Adjust this paragraph to talk about some features of your church building.) We have a beautiful church building. The stones in the building are lovely. Have you ever noticed the ceiling in our sanctuary? It's so high. Let's look at the beams. The beams are in beautiful arches. The windows are colorful and pretty too.

Other churches are beautiful in different ways. Some have very colorful pictures in the windows. Some churches are simple, not decorated much, but still beautiful.

No matter how fancy or simple the church, there is something beautiful about the church that is not the building. Do you know what that might be?

The people in the church make it beautiful! There

are different ways to talk about the word *church*. We talk about the church building. But we also say that the church is the people gathered together.

There is a children's song that tells us about people being a church. The words are: "I am the church. You are the church. We are the church together. All of God's people, all around the world. Yes, we're the church together."

People gathered together worshiping God and caring about one another are the most beautiful and important part of a church.

How many of you know the poem "Here is the church" that you can do with your fingers? Let's do it together. "Here is the church, here is the steeple. Open it up and see all the people." It doesn't matter if the church building is fancy or simple. What matters is the people worshiping God and caring about one another.

Let's pray:

Dear God, we're grateful for our beautiful church building. And we're very grateful for the people gathered in the church, not only here in our church but also all around the world. Amen.

34
The Body of Christ

Theme   We Are All Members of Christ's Body
Scripture   1 Corinthians 12:12-31
Object   Outline of body on paper, pictures
  showing talents people can share

(Gather small pictures showing people sharing their talents; put a circle of tape on the back of each. Make an outline of a body on a piece of paper about the size of child. A larger outline would be unmanageable. Ask a parent to help if you need extra hands.)

GOD WAS VERY CREATIVE when he gave us bodies. We use our fingers, toes, and noses. We use our eyes, mouths, and hearts. Our bodies can do many different things.

There is a part of the Bible that tells about the body of Christ. All of us help to make up the body of Christ. That is hard to imagine, isn't it? The body of Christ is not a body like your body or my body. The body of Christ is all of us joining together and using our special gifts. God gave us all special gifts and talents. Each of us, using these gifts and talents, is needed to make the body of Christ.

I have an outline of a body shape on this paper. I

also have pictures of people using their special talents. These pictures show people singing, helping others, building houses, or doing other projects to serve God.

Each of you will get a picture and place it somewhere on this body outline. Some of the pictures will overlap or touch one another. That's okay. When all the pictures are on the paper, we'll see how we're each needed. Many talents and ways of serving help to make up the body of Christ. After all the pictures are on the body outline, we'll say our prayer. *(This doesn't take long if the tape is on the back of the pictures.)*

Isn't it interesting to see how the people and the ways of serving fill up the body outline? All of us and our talents are needed in the body of Christ.

Let's pray:

Dear God, thank you that we have talents and ways of serving you. Help us to be willing to use these talents. Amen.

35

Keep on Learning

Theme Learning Is a Gift from God
Scripture Proverbs 1:2-9
Object No object, but practice a rhythm pattern

(This can be fun! Practice the poem several times. There are four snaps to each couplet. Before you begin with the children, have them practice the line: "Thanks, God, for helping us learn.")

THIS MORNING I am going to tell you a rhythm poem. But I need your help. There is a line you'll say with me: "Thanks, God, for helping us learn." Then we repeat it, so we're actually saying it twice.

Let's say it together: "Thanks, God, for helping us learn. Thanks, God, for helping us learn."

Good. How many of you can snap your fingers? When I raise my hand, snap your fingers and say the sentences. Let's practice together. Listen to my words and be ready with your line. (* Marks places to snap).

LEADER: *Keeping your *mind awake is* really *fine;
*Keep on *learning; don't *get behind.
There's *so much in* our world to *know;
*gotta keep *learning as *we *grow.

CHILDREN: Thanks, God, for helping us learn.
Thanks, God, for helping us learn.

LEADER: Words to learn, many stories to hear;
we learn something new every day of the year.
Knowing lots about numbers helps us take aim,
so we can keep score at football games.

CHILDREN: Thanks, God, for helping us learn.
Thanks, God, for helping us learn.

LEADER: Playing a game, tying our shoes,
when we keep on learning, there's so much we
can do.
Climbing a tree, and riding a bike,
there's so much to learn that we really like.

CHILDREN: Thanks, God, for helping us learn.
Thanks, God, for helping us learn.

LEADER: Learning about Jesus is really great!
It's good for us to love and not to hate.
We've got to keep learning every single day.
Even when we're grown, there's no better way.

CHILDREN: Thanks, God, for helping us learn.
Thanks, God, for helping us learn.

Let's pray:
Dear God, thank you for giving us minds and a lot
of things to learn. Thank you for parents and teachers
who help us learn. Amen.

36
A Prism for God

Theme   Letting God's Light Shine Through Us
Scripture   2 Corinthians 3:18—4:6
Object   Prism or picture of a prism

GOOD MORNING. Have any of you heard the word *prism* before? That's a word we don't hear often.

A prism is a piece of glass cut in such a way that when light passes through the glass it reflects into many colors. It look like a rainbow dancing on a wall. The light passing through the prism creates something beautiful.

In church and church school, we talk about the light of God. We talk about feeling God with us and in our lives in everything we do. We talk about sharing God's love with other people. We learn about looking for God in the people around us.

Do you know that God's light and love can come from us and help other people? We can be like prisms for God. With God in our lives, we can share with other people the goodness that comes from following God.

As we help other people, we're sharing God's light and love. As we're kind to other people, we're sharing

God's light and love. And as we pray for other people. we're sharing God's light and love.

Maybe sometime you'll see a prism reflecting a beautiful little rainbow on a wall. Remember that you can reflect God's beautiful light and love each day as you follow him. With your families and friends, each day find a special way to share God's light by being caring and loving and helpful.

Let's pray:

Dear God, there are so many beautiful things in our lives. Help us to reflect the beauty of your love to other people. Amen.

37
On Our Journey

Theme We Are All on a Christian Journey

Scripture Galatians 6:1-18

Objects Water bottle, map, sneakers, pretzels, Bible

*H*OW MANY OF YOU like to go for walks? Do you ever go on long walks, with your parents or some friends? You can see many beautiful things on walks. You also need to take some things with you on a walk. *(Bring needed items in bag. Show them one at a time.)*

Let's see what things are needed for a walk.

Sneakers—It's important to wear the right kind of shoes on your walk.

A water bottle—You may get thirsty on your walk, and it's important to take along something to drink.

A snack—Do you get hungry on a walk? Are you hungry right now? I thought so. Each of you may have a handful of pretzels. *(Give each child pretzels.)*

A map—If you're walking on a trail you've never been on before, or if it's really long, it's important to take a map so you don't get lost.

All of these things are important on a walk.

Each of us is on another kind a walk. We're on a

journey because we're Christians. We call it our faith journey.

Just like on a walk through the woods, we need to take some special things along with us on our journey.

We need a Bible. The Bible tells us about Jesus and tells us how we should live our lives. The Bible is like our map.

We need to pray. It's important to talk to Jesus and to listen to know what Jesus wants us to do.

We need friends and family. Those special people can help us on our journey. They can love us, pray for us, and help us. And we can help them.

Having friends, family, prayers, and Jesus in our lives will help guide our journey.

Let's pray:

Dear God, thanks for our friends and family who help us. Thank you that we can help them. Thank you for guiding us on our journey of life. Amen.

38

A Member of Many Families

Theme   We Are Members of Many Families
Scripture   Ephesians 3:17—4:1
Object   Church pictorial directory

*G*OOD MORNING! Tell me, do you like to have your picture taken? Some people do and some people don't. The photographer positions you and tells you to smile. Other people—especially your parents—like to have pictures of you.

I brought our church picture directory with me today. *(Adjust this paragraph to match your pictorial directory.)* There are a lot of special things in this directory. There is a nice picture of the church building. Here are pictures of the church staff. This list tells us who serves on church committees. In the back of the directory are addresses and phone numbers so we know how to contact one another.

But pictures use most of the space in the directory. The pictures show families who are a part of our church. Most of you are pictured in here. *(Pick out pictures of children gathered for story time.)*

Each of us is a member of a family. We each have a

special family. We're also each a member of our church family. Each of us is an important part of our church family. We're also members of a bigger family, members in the kingdom of God.

We use this directory to get to know one another better. We learn people's names and where they live. We learn to recognize people in our church family.

God knows each one of us. But God doesn't need a directory to remember who we are or where we live. God loves us and guides us. God cares for us and helps us. God knows each one of us very well. We're blessed to have our family, our church family, the larger family of God, and God who loves each one of us very much.

Let's pray:

Dear God, thank you for the guidance you give us. Thank you for all of our families—the family we live with, our church family, and your larger family. Amen.

39

*I*ngredients Are Necessary

Theme   We Are Needed in the Church
Scripture   Ephesians 4:11-16
Object   A cookie for each child

*H*OW MANY OF YOU help your mom bake cookies? That's a favorite thing to do! Lots of children like to help bake. Do you know what ingredients are? *(Wait for responses.)*

Ingredients are items needed for a baking project, such as flour, sugar, salt, vanilla, eggs. Some other things are needed too. You mix all these ingredients together after they have been measured.

It's hard to believe the ingredients will turn into cookies! But with the right ingredients and temperatures in the oven, the raw dough will turn into wonderful cookies to eat.

All of the ingredients are necessary for the cookies to turn out right. If the recipe calls for flour and you forget to put it in, the cookies won't bake properly. If your recipe calls for sugar and you forget to put it in, the cookies won't bake properly. All of the ingredients are needed.

We've been talking about ingredients we need for baking cookies. Do you know that each one of us is a necessary ingredient for the church? That's right. Each one of us is needed in the church.

As we learn what our talents are, we should be willing to use them in the church. We're the ingredients of the church. All of us are important.

As we use our talents to sing or read Scripture or show kindness, we're helping the church be great. We're helping God's kingdom to grow. Each one of us is a special ingredient for the church.

I couldn't talk about baking cookies without giving you one, do you think? After our prayer, each of you may take a cookie. As you eat it, remember you're a necessary ingredient for our church.

Let's pray:

Dear God, thank you for giving each one of us many talents. Thank you that there is a special place in our church for each one of us. Amen.

40
*A**ll Over the World*

Theme   Jesus Loves Us All
Scripture   Galatians 3:27-29
Object   Red, yellow, black, white balloons

(Prepare a bouquet of balloons in the following colors—red, yellow, black, and white. Secure the bouquet somewhere in the front of the sanctuary. Afterward give each child a balloon to take home.)

GOOD MORNING! Today is a special day! Do you think so? All days are special. But today is worldwide communion Sunday. That means Christians all over the world are gathering for communion and celebrating being members of the church worldwide.

Worldwide communion Sunday is a special time to remember Jesus' great love for us. We remember how special Jesus is to us and think about how we can serve him in the things we do.

People in other parts of the world might not worship God exactly as we do at our church. People around the world speak many languages. So people worship God in the language they speak best.

People in other parts of the world might use instruments or songs that we don't know when they worship God. But just because they don't sing or use an organ like we do doesn't mean they're not worshiping God.

People don't all have the same color skin. But people with any color of skin can worship God. People worship God in many different ways.

I imagine you're wondering why we have that pretty bouquet of balloons taped to the banister. What colors do you see there? Red, yellow, brown, and white. Do you remember the song "Jesus Loves the Little Children"? The words are, "Jesus loves the little children, all the children of the world. Red, and yellow, brown, and white, they are precious in his sight. Jesus loves the little children of the world."

Jesus does love all of us and we love him. That's a special part of worldwide communion Sunday—saying that we love Jesus. Let's sing that song together. Do you think we should invite the adults to sing with us? Jesus loves them too! *(Sing the song.)*

After the service, come to the front of the church. I'll give each of you one of those special balloons to take home!

Let's pray:

Dear God, thank you for so many different people all over the world. Thank you for your great love for us. We love you, too. Amen.

41
Christians Shouldn't Hibernate

Theme Don't Hibernate with Your Faith

Scripture Mark 13:21-33

Object Picture of bear

GOOD MORNING! We have had a beautiful autumn season, haven't we? Have you noticed the beauty of autumn this year? The leaves have been so colorful. The days have been warm and sunny. The weather has been great for going on walks, going to football games, and doing other fun activities.

Have you noticed the animals preparing for winter? What have you seen? *(Wait for the children to describe some autumn sightings.)*

Some birds have flown south. The squirrels are busy gathering nuts to store for eating during the winter. Some animals are growing thicker fur to give them warm coats for cold winter days.

Some animals are preparing to hibernate. Do you know what *hibernate* means? Some animals sleep most of the winter. They eat a lot before they fall asleep for the winter. Then they don't wake up until early spring. They sleep through the cold months of winter.

Isn't it good that people don't hibernate? Can you imagine sleeping through several months of winter? As Christians, we need to be alert to our actions and stay awake in our relationship with God. We can't let our faith— our trust and belief in God—go to sleep.

We need to keep wide awake to see what God wants us to do. We need to talk to and listen to God through prayer. We can see God in other people. If we take our Christian faith into hibernation, it will be hard to see or hear God. That won't feel good.

There are a lot of ways to keep your relationship with God active. Going to church, reading and listening to Bible stories, singing, praying, and helping other people are all ways of keeping your relationship with God awake.

Don't take your relationship with God into hibernation! Find a way everyday to keep your relationship with God awake!

Let's pray:

Dear God, thanks for our beautiful season of autumn and for the animals that are preparing for winter. Thanks for being with us. Help us to keep our relationship with you awake. Amen.

42

*W*onderful Treasures

Theme We Are Treasures to God
Scripture Ephesians 5:1-2
Object Two stickers for each child

*H*OW MANY OF YOU know what the word *treasure* means? *(Expect a variety of responses—gold, something special under the sea, gifts. Draw the answers into this concluding summary.)* So you tell me that treasures are special things that are kept in a special container.

Do you know that you are treasures to God? Yes, all of us are. Even the grownups! We each have treasures to share with God. When we share our money by placing it in the basket in church school or the offering plate in church, we're sharing treasure with God. The money is used to help with the church's ministry of sharing God with other people.

We give other treasures to God that are not money. When we use our talents—something we're good at— we're sharing treasure with God. Our pastor shares the talent of preaching with us and God. The choir shares their treasure of singing, and that's a gift to God. The organist and pianist share their treasure of music as a gift to God. Everyone in the congregation is sharing a gift with God as we worship him.

I've been telling you mainly of adults sharing treasures. Children have treasures to share too. One big treasure children have to share is smiles. People in our church family often tell me how much they enjoy seeing your smiles when we gather for our story time.

After our prayer together, I am going to give each of you two stickers. Keep one sticker for yourself. Share one sticker with someone else and give that person a smile. By doing that, you're sharing a treasure with someone else and also with God.

Let's pray:

Dear God, you have given us so many treasures— our families, our friends, our homes, and your love are treasures. Thanks, God. Help us to share our treasures with other people while being thankful to you. Amen.

43
Smooth the Rough Edges

Theme   God Smooths Our Rough Edges
Scripture   Philippians 2:1-11
Object   Smooth stone for each child

*T*HIS MORNING I am giving each of you a stone. Please touch and hold it through our story time. *(Pass out the stones.)*

Tell me how these stones feel. *(Expect answers such as cool, light, heavy, smooth. Affirm their answers and work with the idea of the stones being smooth.)*

These stones are smooth. The stones don't have rough edges. That's because they've been in a river where the water has washed over them for a long time and made them smooth.

Sometimes we have rough edges. I don't mean hard or jagged edges like stones might have. But sometimes we're grumpy or angry. Those can be rough edges. Sometimes we worry or lose our patience. Those are like rough edges. Sometimes we're mean and yell at someone or say something we shouldn't. Those are rough edges.

We have rough edges because we all make mistakes. It's natural to feel emotions such as anger or worry because we're human. But when our grumpiness or worry happens so often that it starts harming us or other people, we need to ask God to help us.

When God helps us, that's like having a rough edge smoothed. God can help take away our bad habits. God can help our actions and habits become smooth. God will help us when we ask.

Let's pray:

Dear God, sometimes we do things we shouldn't. Sometimes we get into bad habits. God, we know you can help us to live the way you want us to. Amen.

44

*B*raided Together

Theme God Is with Us
Scripture Ecclesiastes 4:12
Object Three pieces of ribbon to braid

HOW MANY OF YOU know what braiding is? Braiding is weaving three pieces together. Some people wear their hair in braids. *(Look for children in your groups who may have their hair in braids. Mention their names.)* Have any of you braided friendship bracelets? Some people have belts that are braided.

As I'm talking to you this morning, I'm braiding three pieces of ribbon together. When the ribbons are by themselves, they're just single strands. When they're together, they're stronger because they're all woven into a strong braid.

I like to think we're woven together with God. Imagine that the pieces of ribbon are you, other people in our church family, and God. God is woven closely with each us. We're woven together as a church family.

We love one another. We care for and support one another. We help one another. God is woven in with us, too, because God is always present in each person's life. Our prayers to God and listening to God help that weaving together to stay strong.

These were three separate pieces of ribbon. Braided together, they have become one piece. Remember that we also are braided together. Each of us, our church family, and God are braided together as we pray, love, and care for each other.

Let's pray:

Dear God, it's so good to have many people in our church family. Thank you for your presence with us. Thank you that we're strong together. Amen.

45

*F*ollow the Leader

Theme Do As God Instructs Us to Do
Scripture James 1:22-23
Object Bible

GOOD MORNING! How many of you have ever played the game Follow the Leader? Was it fun? Sometimes the leader does easy things—walking in a line or running—that you can follow easily. Sometimes the leader does harder things—jumping or doing somersaults—that are harder to follow but fun to try.

Let's play Follow the Leader this morning. We'll do it sitting here. You do what I do. *(Do simple things like tapping your foot, snapping your fingers, nodding your head.)* Now let's say together, "God, I want to follow you." Ready? "God, I want to follow you."

Do you know that God is the best leader we can have? God wants all of us to follow him.

We can learn what God wants us to do from the Bible. In the Bible we learn how to be good people. We learn that God wants us to care for other people and tell them of his love.

We can learn what we are supposed to do from the Bible, but then we need to do those things. It's not enough just to know what God wants us to do. We're actually supposed to do those things—being kind and helpful, living a life that shows God to other people.

In a game of Follow the Leader, it's not fun to stand back and watch everyone else play. In our lives, it's much better to follow God and do what God wants us to do because God is the best leader we can have.

Let's pray:

Dear God, thank you so much for being the best leader we can have. We want to follow you and do what's right and good. Guide us as we follow you. Amen.

46

Someone Is at the Door

Theme Jesus Wants to Be in Our Lives
Scripture Revelation 3:20
Object Picture of Jesus knocking at a door

*H*OW MANY OF YOU have a doorbell at your house? When you hear it ring, do you run to see who is there? Maybe it's a grandparent, or a friend, or a special delivery. Do you ever ring it just for fun?

I have a picture to show you today. It shows Jesus knocking at a door. Some of our church school classrooms have this picture on the wall. Jesus is patiently knocking at the door. Jesus isn't ringing a doorbell. Do you notice there isn't even a doorknob on the door? There is no way Jesus can open the door and walk in. Jesus needs to wait until someone opens the door. Jesus is just patiently knocking, waiting for someone to let him in.

There is a verse in the Bible that says, "Listen! I am standing at the door knocking; if you hear my voice, and open the door, I will come in to you and eat with you, and you with me."

Jesus wants to be part of our lives. Jesus waits for us to say, "Jesus, I want you to be part of my life." It's like Jesus is knocking at our door saying, "I would like to come in to stay with you."

Jesus loves each of us and wants to be a special part of our lives. Knowing that Jesus would like to be an important part of our lives is special. The best part is knowing that Jesus will never leave us. No thing or person can take Jesus away from us.

Let's pray:

Dear Jesus, thank you for wanting to be part of our lives. We're glad for that. Amen.

47
T hanks, God

Theme God Has Given Us Wonderful Gifts
Scripture James 1:17
Object Pictures illustrating thankfulness

(Prepare a book using pictures from magazines or family photos to illustrate the phrases in this poem. Put them together in a three-ring notebook. Put each phrase on a different page in the notebook. At the end of your time together, encourage the children to make a similar book of things for which they are thankful.)

T HANKS, God, for so many things,
each new day and all it brings;
  our families filled with love and care,
our houses and all the laughter there;
  for all the food we have to eat,
meat and vegetables, fruits and sweets;
  for friends with whom we have so much fun,
in spring, winter, fall, and summer sun.
  Thanks for all the times we find rest,
nights, weekends, and vacations are the best!
  Thank you for cultural exposure,
sports, books, and Beethoven's overtures.
  There's so much to learn, not just in school;

keeping our minds awake is really cool.

Thanks, God, for the world around
where so much beauty does abound:

sunshine and rain, grass and trees,
farms and gardens, flowers and bees.

Thanks for all the ways we can travel,
over roads, mountains, highways, or gravel,

feet, cars, bikes, trains,
trucks, planes, and rollerblades.

Thank you, God, for Jesus your Son.
His example is great when it is all said and done.

Thanks, God, for all your gifts, and for all you do,
But, God, most of all, thanks for being you!

Let's pray:

Dear God, you have given us so many gifts. Thank you very much! Amen.

48

Let's Have a Closer Look

Theme   We Celebrate the Birth of Jesus
Scripture   Luke 2:1-7
Object   Magnifying glass, tiny picture,
Christmas cards or Advent calendars

(Prepare a picture of Mary and baby Jesus by using a Xerox machine to reduce a picture from a Christmas card until a magnifying glass is needed to identify it. However, be careful not to reduce it to such a small picture that it frustrates the children. Depending on how many children will be there, you may want to have one or two extra people with the same picture and a magnifying glass. I had two extra people.)

GOOD MORNING! We all know that we use our eyes to see. What are some things that help us to see better? *(Affirm the children's answers. You might expect the following—glasses, sunglasses, contact lenses. Guide their thinking to a magnifying glass.)*

A telescope helps us to see things far away. A microscope helps us to see tiny things. What does a magnifying glass do? It also helps us to see tiny things. When we are looking for something, a magnifying glass sometimes helps.

I have a magnifying glass with me this morning. I

also have something to look at. Everyone will get a chance to see. Let's wait until everyone has had a chance to look before we say what we have seen. *(Let the children try to identify the pictures. Use your helpers now if you need them.)*

Okay. Everyone has had a chance to see. What's in the picture? You're right! Mary and baby Jesus.

At this time of year we think about Christmas and the birth of Jesus. In the midst of all the special things we can do at Christmastime, sometimes it's easy for us to forget that we're celebrating Jesus' birthday.

We have trees, presents, lights, and cookies, and other special things. However, sometimes we need to take time to remember that Jesus is the reason for Christmas. It's almost as if we need a magnifying glass to help us see what we're supposed to be celebrating.

To help you remember the real meaning of Christmas, I'm going to give each of you a card *(or calendar)* with a picture of Mary and baby Jesus on it. *(I gave the children Advent calendars.)* Keep it with you this Christmas season. Put it by your bed, or on your dresser, or on your refrigerator—wherever you like as long as you let it remind you of Jesus.

Let's pray:

Dear God, thank you for the birth of Jesus. Help us to think a lot about Jesus during the Christmas season. Amen.

49
The Long Wait

Theme Have Some Christmas Every Day
Scripture James 5:7-8
Object Front page of newspaper counting the
days till Christmas

(Most newspapers have a countdown to Christmas some-where in the paper. Begin your time with the children by guiding their thoughts to the Christmas countdown.)

I BROUGHT THE FRONT page of the newspaper with me today. We can learn a lot of things from the front page. What all do you think we can learn? *(Expect answers such as headline news, weather, index of contents.)*

You're right. We can learn all those things. In the days before Christmas, our paper also has a special picture on the front page. Can you find it?

There it is. It's a special comic strip counting the days until Christmas. Yesterday it was ____ days. So that means Christmas is how many days from today? You're right!

Sometime it's hard to wait until Christmas. We know that exciting things await us like fun time with family, special things to do, and exchanging presents.

But we also know that Christmas is about something more important. We remember that Jesus came to us as a baby and we celebrate his birthday. There is a song that says, "Love came down at Christmas time." That means God showed us a lot of love when Jesus was born.

We can show love to the people around us. That doesn't mean we need to wait until Christmas Day to show that love. We can show love every day, and by sharing that love, we have a little piece of Christmas every day.

As we count down the days until Christmas, whether we check the front page of the paper or watch a calendar, let's each remember to share some Christmas love each day.

Let's pray:
Dear God, thanks for all of your love and for sending Jesus to us. Help us to show some Christmas love each day. Amen.

50
Share a Christmas Card

Theme Share a Card to Help Share Christmas
  Hope
Scripture Isaiah 11:1-10
Object Christmas card and envelope for each
  child to share with someone else

(Prepare a Christmas card and envelope for each child to receive to share with someone else, thereby sharing the hope of Christmas.)

GOOD MORNING! We have just a couple of weeks until Christmas! This is a busy and fun time of year! What is your family doing to prepare? *(Be prepared for enthusiastic responses. Affirm answers and guide thinking to sending and receiving Christmas cards.)*

Some families are mailing Christmas cards. Have you gotten Christmas cards in the mail yet?

It's fun to open cards to see who they're from. It's also special to read holiday greetings inside cards. Here are some verses from cards we've received. *(Have a slip of paper on which you've written three or four holiday greetings and read them.)*

Christmas cards are a nice way to share a Christmas greeting with other people. By sharing a Christmas greeting, we share love and good wishes.

Most of you probably don't pick cards your family sends, parents usually do. When people choose cards, they usually read the verse to see if they like it.

One woman was in a hurry at Christmas! She bought cards that had the same verse on each card. She didn't read the verse. She mailed the cards and had two left.

Later, she read the extra cards. The verse on the card said, "Keep your eyes open; watch everyday, a gift from me is coming your way!"

She had told everyone she sent a card to that she would send a gift. She couldn't keep that promise.

By sending cards with special messages, we share the hope that comes to us at Christmas. To help you share that hope, I'll give you a card and an envelope. The message on the card says _____. *(Read the message from the cards you will be giving the children.)*

This card is for you to give to someone. Ask your mom or dad to help you address it, if you need help. Maybe you could give it to your teacher or your bus driver if you go to school. Maybe you could give it to a neighbor or your babysitter.

Find someone with whom to share the hope of Christmas, write your name on the card, and give it to that person. You will be sharing the hope of Christmas.

Let's pray:

Dear God, thank you for the hope you give to us by being with us every day. Thank you for the birth of Jesus, which gives us hope and joy. Amen.

51

J esus in Our Lives

Theme   Let Others See Jesus in Your Lives
Scripture   Luke 2:1-7
Object   Manger scene with a constructed cradle enclosing a mirror

(This story time requires a bit of easy preparation. Use a small, cardboard jewelry box and cut the bottom out of it. Secure a mirror in it. Then glue a little dried grass around the box to give the appearance of a manger. At a point in the story, the children will look into the mirror and see themselves.)

GOOD MORNING! Christmas Day is coming soon! In the past few weeks, we have been celebrating Advent by lighting the candles, saying special prayers, and singing special Christmas songs. Today, let's set up a manger scene together. *(Place the manger scene objects as you mention them. Don't put the manger in place.)*

In the Christmas story we hear about the stable where Jesus was born. We know that Mary, Joseph, and some animals were there. We hear about shepherds who came to visit because they saw angels and a star in the sky. We hear about wise men who traveled far to bring gifts to Jesus. There we go. Is it all in place?

(Wait for the children's response.)

It's not? Is something missing? You're right! The manger with Jesus. I have it with me, but I want you to look into it first. What do you see? Yourself.

There is a song that says, "You're the only Jesus some may ever see." Wow! We know that Jesus came to our world as a baby to bring peace, hope, and love. We can share that peace, hope, and love with other people. We know that Jesus sets the best example for us to follow.

Let's all try to live our lives in a way that shows that Jesus lives with us. We hope that through our words and actions, people will see Jesus in us.

Let's pray:

Dear God, thanks for Christmas. Thanks for Jesus who came as a baby to bring peace, hope, and love to our world. We pray to live our lives in ways that other people will see Jesus in us. Amen.

52

The Simple Manger

Theme Jesus Had a Simple Beginning
Scripture Luke 2:1-7
Object Manger scene (including a stable)

GOOD MORNING! Happy Christmas! This is the Sunday before Christmas. All of us have been busy getting ready for Christmas Day.

In the midst of the busyness, have you been remembering who's birthday we are celebrating? *(Hope to get a positive response!)* Good for you! During our story time together, let us talk about the birth of Jesus.

(Place the stable where all children can see it.) We hear that Jesus was born in a stable. What do you imagine a stable was like? *(Expect answers such as cold, smelly, dusty.)*

A stable is a rather unlikely place for a special king like Jesus to be born. It doesn't seem like a baby should be born in a dusty building and surrounded by animals, does it? *(Add the nativity figures as you speak. Adjust this paragraph to match the pieces in your nativity set.)*

The only place Mary and Joseph could find to stay was in the stable. There was no other place for them to rest. Well, as you know, something wonderful happened in that stable. Amidst the animals, the coolness, and the dust, Jesus was born.

Mary and Joseph were happy. They were probably tired from their long journey, but they were happy that the baby was born and was healthy.

A star appeared in the sky and angels began to sing. The star acted as a guide for people to come to the stable. Shepherds came to say they were glad Jesus was born. And kings came on camels carrying such treasures such as gold, frankincense, and myrrh to say that they were glad Jesus was born.

Because of that wonderful night, we can have Jesus in our lives. Jesus was born in an unlikely place, the manger, for us. That is the best gift! As we celebrate Christmas, remember that Jesus is the best gift ever given to any of us.

Let's pray:

Dear God, thank you for the wonderful Christmas story. Thank you for Jesus, who is a great gift to us. Amen.

The Author

Donna McKee Rhodes, a licensed minister in the Church of the Brethren, is presently minister of nurture at the Stone Church of the Brethren, Huntingdon, Pa. Donna is a 1984 graduate of Juniata College with a B.S. in early childhood and elementary education. She is also a graduate of the Church of the Brethren Training in Ministry program and has pursued additional studies at Bethany Theological Seminary.

Donna's Christian education ministry has included being a teacher, consultant, developer of educational material, and author. She has written *Little Stories for Little Children* (Herald Press, 1995), which won a Silver Angel award. She is a writer for *Jubilee! God's Good News*, the curriculum for children in Anabaptist churches.

Donna was born in Mifflin Country, Pa. She now lives in Huntingdon, Pa., with her husband Loren, a professor of computer science at Juniata College, and their children Erica (1984), Aaron (1986), and Joel (1991). Donna enjoys music, crafts, reading, and the activities of her children.